G000294356

CONTENTS

INTRO

FIRST OFF, WELL DONE!

MAKING IT TO university in the first place is no mean feat. So congratulations on getting through the endless rewrites of your personal statement, all that revision, the exam stress, the tearful farewells and the shopping for a toaster. Allow yourself a satisfied smile for a moment. University is brilliant. It'll stretch your mind and your faith, teach you loads about yourself and God, not to mention the subject you're studying, and could give you friends for life. We hope the *Mettle Guide to Starting University* will give you some wise and practical advice on how to make the most of your university experience. It won't answer all your questions or give you a simple formula for how to be simultaneously a brilliant student *and* a brilliant Christian, but we hope it will at least give you a nudge in the right direction. After that, it's over to you ...

1

SECTION

M

HAVING THE RIGHT FRIENDS IS IMPORTANT. THE FIRST
SECTION OF THE GUIDE WILL LOOK AT EXACTLY WHO THE
'RIGHT FRIENDS' ARE AND HOW TO HOLD ON TO THEM.

ATES

YOUR
MATES

TIP 1

Talk to absolutely anyone! – University is a chance to meet all kinds of people. Not everyone will be like you, but that's the beauty of it. There will be people around you from all manner of different backgrounds, with different experiences, different views, different skills and different faiths. There are all manner of stimulating and mind-broadening conversations to be had and you might be surprised which people you find yourself connecting with. Don't hide in your room. Get out there and meet some people!

TIP 2

Choose your friends wisely – Talking to absolutely anyone isn't the same as being friends with absolutely anyone. It's worth making wise decisions about who you really want as your friends. In Freshers' Week, it may be tempting to gravitate towards the people who seem to be having the most fun, but is that what *really* matters in a friend? Find people who will be wise, loyal and supportive; who will stick with you for the long-term, even if they seem like oddballs to start with.

130

130 – NUMBER OF FACEBOOK FRIENDS THE AVERAGE USER HAS

TIP 3

Stay in touch with your old friends – If everything's going well, your first term should be a blast. With all the people you're meeting, fun you're having, clubs you're joining and stuff you're studying, it's easy to forget about the people you've left behind. It's worth staying in touch with friends at home or at other unis though. They've been good friends and stuck with you so far and they're likely to stay that way for many years to come, if you make the effort to stay in touch *now*. With Facebook, Skype and text messaging available to you, there's really no excuse ...

KEY VERSE v26 'The godly give good advice to their friends; the wicked lead them astray.'

CHOOSING YOUR FRIENDS wisely can make a massive difference to your university experience. Good friends will give you good advice, support you and stick with you when life gets tough. On the other hand, just drifting into friendships with the wrong people can land you in all sorts of trouble. I was lucky enough to have some brilliant friends at uni. We had a lot of fun together, but they were also there for me when life wasn't so good. I don't know how I would have coped with my finals without them. We're still in touch now, ten years after graduating and I'm so glad we've stayed friends. At the opposite extreme, we all come across people who just want to take advantage of us, borrow money and never pay it back, or use our stuff without asking.

These verses from Proverbs give us a checklist of qualities to look for in a friend. Does this person tell the truth (v.22)? Do they work hard, rather than expecting other people to do everything for them (v.24)? Do they support you and encourage you (v.25)? Are they wise about how they use money and possessions (v.27)? And perhaps most importantly, do they want what's best for you and give you wise advice (v.26)? If you can answer 'yes' to those questions, then you've probably got a friend worth hanging on to. If you're answering 'no' more than once, perhaps you should think again about whether you want this person influencing you.

Especially in Freshers' Week, you'll be surrounded by all sorts of interesting people. It can be tempting to just hang around with the people who seem to be having the most fun. Not that there's anything wrong with having fun, of course, but that probably isn't the wisest way of choosing your friends. If you're not sure about which of the people around you would be good friends, pray about this whole issue. God is the best Friend we'll ever have – the one Person we can absolutely rely on to help us and advise us. He wants each of us to have good friends, and He can show you who you should choose to spend time with, if you ask Him.

 THINK

Which of the people around you are real friends to you? Are you choosing your friends wisely?

READING 1 Thessalonians 3:6–13

KEY VERSE
v11 'May God our Father and our Lord Jesus bring us to you very soon.'

DAY 02

14

WHEN I STARTED at university, I had to move from London to York. It meant leaving a lot of good friends behind, including people who'd really encouraged me in my faith. I was worried about how I'd cope without them and concerned whether we'd even keep in touch. It wasn't easy to say goodbye, but I knew it was right for me to go.

I think Paul would have understood how I felt. These verses give us a very powerful impression of how much he cares about the Christians in Thessalonica and how much he misses them. His words to them are a real encouragement that God is still with us and with our friends, even when we're not together, and that He has plans for each of us. Paul also challenges us to keep praying for our friends and building them up in their faith, however far away they are.

When you start at university and find yourself surrounded by new people, it can be tempting to invest all your time in them and forget about your old friends. This is a mistake! If we make the effort to keep in touch with friends back home or at different universities, we're likely to find, as Paul did, that our spirits are lifted and that there is a lot to be thankful for.

I needn't have worried about staying in touch with my friends. They kept sending me letters and emails all the way through my time at uni. (This was in the good old days before Facebook!) I still saw them when I was home for the holidays too. Your best friends will almost certainly stay in touch with you. But it's also up to you to keep up *your* end of the relationship. (Beware the opposite danger: spending so much time on the phone or Facebook with your friends back home that you lose sight of what's going on around you now!) Staying connected to your old friends will encourage you, inspire you and, if your friends are Christians, be a big help in your walk with God.

PRAY

Pray for any friends you're leaving behind or who are at uni somewhere else. Make Paul's prayer your own: 'May the Lord make your love for one another and for all people grow and overflow, just as our love for you overflows. May he, as a result, make your hearts strong, blameless, and holy as you stand before God our Father when our Lord Jesus comes again with all his holy people. Amen.'

KEY VERSE
v13 'There is no greater love than to lay down one's life for one's friends.'

I LOOK BACK at how I behaved at university and I cringe. I was lazy, self-absorbed, self-righteous and stingy. I particularly feel sorry for the poor people who had to share a house with me! So it's remarkable that some of the people who were my friends then are still my friends now. However clueless and anti-social my behaviour was, they stuck with me. When I was ill or homesick or stressed about coursework, they were always there for me. I can only hope I've been as much of a faithful friend to them over the years as they've been to me.

Jesus makes it clear that self-sacrifice is a crucial part of true friendship. He Himself modelled this in everything He did, constantly putting other people's needs before His own. And in the end, Jesus gave us the ultimate example of self-sacrifice by choosing to die so that His friends would be free from sin and free to know God. I hope that none of us will find ourselves in a position where we have to choose to *literally* die for our friends, but there's no doubt that all of us will at times have to choose whether to put our friends' needs before our own. In fact, at uni, we'll probably face several of these decisions every day. Will I help my housemates do the washing up or sit and watch TV? Will I spend time cheering up my friend who's feeling down, or just go out to the union bar? Will I cook tonight, or let someone else do it again? These little decisions can have a big impact on our friendships.

That's not to say that we should be doormats and let our friends walk all over us and take advantage of us. But our attitude towards our friends is very important. We must be willing to serve them, to put *their* needs before our own. Above all, just as the friends I made at university stuck with me, we should stick with our friends, even if they're a bit annoying at times.

 ### CHALLENGE

Is one of your friends winding you up? Perhaps this person is a bit lazy and self-absorbed, like I was. Pray for this person and resolve to be patient and stick with them. Then do something to show this person that you're there for them. Remember how patient God is with each of us, whatever we do.

KEY VERSE v14 'You are the light of the world – like a city on a hilltop that cannot be hidden.'

THERE ARE TOO many Christians out there who go through life in 'holy huddles'. All their friends are Christians, all the stuff they do in their spare time is with Christians, they only listen to 'Christian' music and they might even only work with Christians! Unfortunately, universities have Christians like this too. Don't get me wrong, it's very important to have Christian friends who can encourage you in your faith, but if you *only* have Christian friends, something is wrong.

Living in a holy huddle seems to be mostly motivated by a fear of being 'polluted' in some way by the sin in the world around us. A number of people in Jesus' time thought a similar way. (A group of people called the Essenes chose to live in the desert, so that they'd never have to see anyone else, and they'd therefore avoid being corrupted by what they saw as the sin and godlessness in their culture.) But Jesus turns this way of thinking on its head. Instead of worrying about being influenced in a negative way by the world, Jesus urges us to be the ones who influence the world in a positive way. Jesus has made us the 'light of the world'. We carry His presence with us wherever we go. His light,

His goodness, His love and His truth shine through us and affect the people around us. Of course, for this to happen, we need to actually spend time with people who don't already know Jesus!

There are so many ways to do this! Join a few clubs and societies and influence them in a godly way. Get involved in student politics and campaign for God-inspired change in your university. Or just spend time with people from your halls or your course. Don't be afraid of being 'corrupted' in some way by campus life. Instead, be the light of the world in your university and make it a little bit more like the kingdom of God. Open your eyes to what God wants to do and is already doing around you, and choose to be a part of that.

THINK

What do you think God wants to do at your university? Who can you spend time with? Which clubs or societies could you join? How can you be 'the light of the world' at your uni and make it a little more like the kingdom of God?

 **KEY VERSE v2** 'Don't copy the behavior and customs of this world, but let God transform you into a new person by changing the way you think.'

DAY 05

20

NONE OF US notice the air around us. Why would we? We're so used to it being there that we just breathe it in and get on with life. Unfortunately, we often have the same attitude towards the culture we live in. We're used to our culture being there, so we just accept it and get on with life. The trouble is, like the air we breathe, our culture affects us deeply. If there are problems within our culture, they can affect us without us realising. For example, if people around us drink too much, sleep around and value possessions more than people, we can drift into the same patterns of behaviour. This can be particularly true at university, where there's little escape from campus life and where we're amongst a group of people with some deeply ingrained attitudes and behaviours.

We all know that our lifestyle is crucial to our faith. Following Jesus isn't just about believing and saying the right things; it's about our actions too. So we must be aware of the ways in which our culture influences our behaviour. If we mentally take a step back and look at the way people around us are behaving, we can get an insight into what aspects of this are at odds with how God would want us to act. Paul (who wrote Romans) urges us, 'Don't copy the behavior and customs of this world' (v.2). This doesn't mean we should retreat into some kind of Christian ghetto, where the secular culture can't reach us. But it does mean that while we live in this secular culture, we need to be aware of what's unhelpful about it, and not just go along with the same unhealthy behaviour our friends might be caught up in. It's also worth being accountable to one or two Christian friends, who can help keep us on track.

I'm sure you can already think of examples of behaviour which would be best avoided. But there's another angle to explore too. Jesus doesn't just want us to draw up a list of stuff to avoid. He wants us to be His witnesses in our culture and on our campuses. That means actively doing things that please Him, even if nobody else seems to be doing them. And how do we know what Jesus would want us to do? We spend time with Him, we pray and we let Him change the way we think, and transform us.

PRAY

Spend some time praying about this issue now. Ask God to change the way you think, transform you and help you behave wisely in the culture He's put you in.

'Run from sexual sin! No other sin so clearly affects the body as this one does. For sexual immorality is a sin against your own body.'

IF WE LOOK at what's going on around us and listen to some of what people we know are talking about, it can seem like anything goes as far as sex is concerned. Our friends might be having sex with strangers (or at least claiming they're doing that) or exploring a homosexual lifestyle, for example. All this can leave us feeling as if we're missing out in some way if we're not behaving like this.

Actually, it's true. We are missing out. We're missing out on sexually transmitted infections and unwanted pregnancies. We're missing out on feeling used when the person we slept with last night doesn't want to know us in the morning. We're missing out on the insecurity that comes from wondering how we compare with the other person's previous sexual partners.

God speaks to us not just in this reading from 1 Corinthians but throughout the Bible and urges us to save sex for the one person we marry. He doesn't do that to spoil our fun or limit our experience. He wants us to save sex for marriage because He wants to save us from a lot of physical and emotional pain. God created sex to be the ultimate expression of love; a joyful experience to enrich an already deeply committed relationship between two people. If we choose to 'run from sexual sin', it doesn't make us killjoys. It just means we value sex, ourselves and the people we'll later marry too highly to compromise.

Make a conscious decision to save sex for the person you marry. Don't just avoid having sex with anyone in the meantime; avoid doing anything that even looks like becoming 'sexual sin'! This won't always be easy with plenty of good looking people and a lot of temptation around you, but it's definitely the wisest attitude towards sex and with God's help, you can do it. And why is everyone so obsessed with having a boyfriend or girlfriend anyway? Spend your first couple of terms at uni investing in friendships. There's plenty of time to develop dating relationships later on.

THINK

What can you do to make sure you don't give in to sexual temptation? How can you help your non-Christian friends to understand why you're saving sex for marriage? Is there anything around this issue for which you need to ask God to forgive you? Do you need to change your focus from casual dating to building lasting friendships?

KEY VERSE 'A friend is always loyal, and a brother
v17 is born to help in time of need.'

FRESHERS' WEEK IS brilliant. There are loads of
people to meet, there's stuff to do and fun to be had.
But once the dust has settled on Freshers' Week
and the initial excitement of uni life fades, you may
find that not everything is quite as brilliant as you
first thought. Your course might turn out to be not
quite what you expected. Your flatmates might start
winding you up. Or you might just start missing
your family and old friends. At some stage in our
time at university, all of us will face at least one or
two things that make us upset, angry or depressed.
Money, relationships and coursework are the biggest
culprits. At times like these, how we handle our
struggles is all important.

In my second term at uni, my gran died. I was
pretty upset about this, but just bottled it up and
didn't talk to anyone. I ended up feeling very low and
quite isolated. Looking back, things would have been
so much better if I'd just talked to one of my friends.
I would have *felt* better and my relationships with
one or more of my friends would have become more
meaningful. It probably sounds obvious, but talking to

someone when you're struggling is definitely the best way forward. I've learned the hard way that bottling things up just isn't good for you. God has created us to be relational; to care for and support each other. He's put your friends around you precisely for the times when you're at your lowest.

Talk to someone if you're struggling. This could be one of your uni friends or someone back home. And if you really don't want to talk to someone you know about your problem, most universities have some kind of phone advice line or counselling service. But whatever you do, talk to someone and share your struggle. And we can always pray too. God, after all, is the best Friend we'll ever have (Prov. 18:24) and understands all our struggles (Heb. 4:14–16).

PRAY

If you're struggling with a problem, pray about it now. If you're feeling fine, pray for someone you know who has a problem. Also ask God to put people around you who you can really trust and talk to. Why not think about volunteering with your uni's student advice line, if there is one?

MY STORY

I VIDLY REMEMBER the day I met Tony. The chaplain's invitation to tea and free cakes was too tempting for either of us to miss. So we bumped into each other, almost literally, as we found we were heading the same way.

Tony and I just clicked. His unconditional love, brilliant sense of humour and acceptance of people were inspirational – and his love for God infectious.

I've never had such varied friends as those I knew that first year on campus: Christians and atheists; scientists, poets, musicians, historians, linguists; and a friend, Charlie, with physical disabilities and a radiant Catholic faith. (We, on the corridor, needed to feed Charlie and occasionally put him back into bed if he fell out, yet he had his own university radio show, drove a car and went on to obtain a First.) My gay friends varied between those who were passionately gay and those who were passionate Christians, struggling to resolve issues relating to their sexuality.

Sharing a house off-campus with Tony and others in my third year was never dull: an eccentric Maths student from our corridor, found sleeping in a bathroom during his retakes, shared Tony's bedroom during Tony's finals. Visitors often left the meal table convulsed with laughter, and occasionally addressed 'thank you' notes to us as 'The family at Thief Lane'.

To say that my university friendships were formative and life-changing is almost an understatement. Two of those friends, one being Tony, asked me: 'Will you still be my friend "When I'm 64"?' (a line from a Beatles song). We are still friends – and have only another 12 years to go!

Carol, Language graduate
and freelance writer

SECTION $\frac{2}{\Box}$

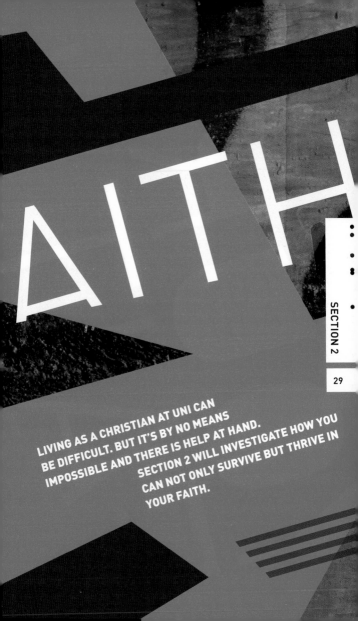

AITH

LIVING AS A CHRISTIAN AT UNI CAN BE DIFFICULT. BUT IT'S BY NO MEANS IMPOSSIBLE AND THERE IS HELP AT HAND. SECTION 2 WILL INVESTIGATE HOW YOU CAN NOT ONLY SURVIVE BUT THRIVE IN YOUR FAITH.

YOUR
FAITH

TIP 1

Find a church – This is important. Too many Christians move away to uni, don't bother finding a church, drift along as lone-ranger Christians for three years and end up losing their faith. Don't try to go it alone. God designed us to be in relationships with other people. A church will encourage us when we're down, share our joy when everything's great, give us wisdom and direction and be a safe place to ask questions. It's also somewhere you can give something back, help other people and find out a bit more about what your gifts are. The Christian Union is very important too, but make sure you find a church.

TIP 2

Develop good habits – Being a Christian doesn't just mean thinking good 'Christian' thoughts and being nice to people. If you're serious about wanting to follow Jesus and know Him better, there's no substitute for building some simple disciplines into your life. Spend some time every day reading your Bible and praying. There's no 'right' way of doing this, so find a time of day and method that work for you. There are other disciplines to learn, but get this one licked and the others tend to follow.

70 –
ESTIMATED
PERCENTAGE
OF CHRISTIAN
STUDENTS
WHO DO NOT
ATTEND
CHURCH
REGULARLY

TIP 3

Work out what you believe and why – If someone asks you what you think of smoking weed or having sex before marriage, just saying, 'I think it's wrong' won't cut it. You can bet that the follow-up question will be 'Why?' and you'll need to be ready with an answer. There will be a lot of people around who are genuinely interested in what you believe and will find it quite frustrating if it looks like you haven't thought it through. Don't be afraid to grapple with some awkward questions about God and life in general. If Jesus is the Way, the Truth and the Life (which He is), then your faith won't fall apart if you kick the tyres a little. In fact, you're likely to grow through the process.

READING Mark 1:35–39

 KEY VERSE
v35 'Before daybreak the next morning, Jesus got up and went out to an isolated place to pray.'

WHEN WE'RE BUSY, praying and reading the Bible can often be the first things to go. In your first term at uni, there will be so much stuff to do: people to meet, lectures to go to and essays to write, not to mention all the partying. In all the excitement, it's very easy for spending time with God to be squeezed out. When that happens, it usually isn't a conscious decision; it just gets forgotten. We might even find that it's important and godly stuff that makes us busy: CU committee meetings, social action projects or RAG fundraising. We can make ourselves so busy doing 'the work of the Lord' that we forget the Lord of the work!

The disciples seemed surprised and exasperated that Jesus felt the need to spend so long praying, when there was so much work to do (v.37). Perhaps Jesus got a new sense of energy and purpose from spending time with His Father. It certainly seems that way from verses 38–39. Immediately after praying, Jesus has a very clear idea of where He needs to go and what He should do. For Jesus, praying wasn't a distraction from His ministry: praying made His ministry possible and added life, energy and vision to it. For sure, Jesus saw it as essential to spend time praying. No matter how busy He was or however many people were looking for Him, He put His relationship with God first. The challenge for us is obvious: we should put our relationship with God first too.

This doesn't necessarily mean getting up before dawn to pray (although that can be a useful habit!). But it definitely does mean *consciously* setting aside time to pray and read your Bible. The best way of doing that is to get into a routine, praying at the same time every day. It'll make sure God doesn't get crowded out by all the 'stuff to do'. By all means make yourself busy, but don't be too busy to pray.

 CHALLENGE

Look at your calendar now. Set aside time every day to pray and read your Bible. Mark this on your calendar. Then stick to it! Let nothing else interrupt this time. Perhaps find another Christian who's trying to do the same thing and encourage each other in this. Keep checking how the other person is doing and ask them to do the same for you.

READING Hebrews 10:19–25

 KEY VERSE
v25
'... let us not neglect our meeting together, as some people do, but encourage one another ...'

DAY 09

36

PERHAPS, LIKE ME, you have friends who are Christians but who don't see the point in going to church. Perhaps you even feel that way yourself. After all, particularly if your church services are a bit dull, how is it helping you? Wouldn't you be better off just staying in bed on Sunday mornings? Well, it can be very frustrating if your church services are a bit uninspiring, but to stop going to church because of that is rather missing the point. Church isn't about being entertained. Church is about a group of people who are committed to Jesus and committed to each other. Church should strengthen us in our faith and also be God's agent to change our communities. This can only happen if we're in the habit of meeting with the other members of our church. That's what church services are for.

When I look back at the times in my life when things have got tough, it's been my friends from church who have encouraged me and helped me. When I was at university, I had friends both from my church and from the Christian Union who supported me and spurred me on in my faith. When I think of my friends who have turned their backs on church, when life got hard for them they found they'd drifted away from the people who would have helped them. When we're in trouble, we really start to see the benefit of belonging to a church. Even if you can't see the benefit right now, stick with it. And don't forget that you have a duty to build up and support other people in your church too!

It's also very important to get involved with other Christians on campus through your Christian Union. Your CU will provide opportunities to grow in your faith and get to know other Christians, who understand the pressures of uni life and can support you in it. The Christian Union isn't a substitute for joining a church. Both communities are valuable and important. Being part of a church will be a constant reminder that not all Christians are students! It will keep you connected to believers of all ages and backgrounds. A Christian Union will make you a part of a network of people who are trying to live out their faith on campus, just like you. Belonging to both groups will help you develop a healthy, balanced faith.

 THINK

How can your church and CU help you? How can you help them? If you need help connecting with a CU or a church, UCCF (www.uccf.org.uk) and Fusion (www.fusion.uk.com) can help you.

KEY VERSE 'Those who are the greatest among
v26 you should take the lowest rank, and
the leader should be like a servant.'

I WENT TO university in York. York is a small city
and seems to have a very high number of homeless
people for a city of its size. Someone in my Christian
Union noticed how many homeless people there
were in the city and decided we should do something
to help them. She hit on the idea of getting a team
of people together, once a week, to take coffee and
sandwiches to some of the people on the streets and
to sit and talk to them. We got some funny looks,
sitting in doorways, talking to these guys, and it made
me quite self-conscious, but I believe this is exactly
the kind of thing Jesus would have done.

Jesus and His disciples would have seen a lot of
political and religious leaders who loved to posture,
make themselves look good and order people around.
In fact, Roman emperors insisted on being worshipped
as gods. Jesus completely rejects this concept of
greatness. Even though Jesus was God in human form
and deserved to be worshipped, He humbled Himself
and came to serve (v.27). Jesus even served Judas,
who He knew was going to betray Him. Jesus shows
us that true greatness isn't about looking good or
ordering people around; it's about serving people.
He challenges us to follow His example.

You will know better than I do who around you needs to be served. It could be the homeless people in your town. It could be international students who are feeling lonely and homesick. It could just be someone on your corridor who's struggling with a problem. Whatever the need, Jesus' challenge to serve is as important as ever while we're at university. We mustn't become so absorbed in coursework and partying that we forget that. And don't try to go it alone on this. Get involved with what your CU is already doing to serve people, or get them on board with your ideas. There are charities that can help you serve people in need too. Do some research and see who are real experts in this area.

PRAY

Think about who around you needs to be helped in some way. Make a list if it helps. Then pray through the list, asking God to help each of these people and to show you how *you* can be part of that. Then do what you can to serve the people you prayed for, in Jesus' name.

READING Acts 1:1–11

 KEY VERSE '... you will be my witnesses, telling
v8 people about me everywhere ....'

I WONDER HOW the disciples felt when they heard these words. Perhaps they were excited about the possibilities; all the people who they would tell about Jesus and who would then want to follow Him. I suspect they were afraid too, though. Jesus was no longer physically with them and it was up to them to continue His work and share His message with people who not long before had killed Jesus and threatened His followers.

The concept of sharing our faith can be daunting for us too. I have vivid memories of being the only Christian amongst a group of friends sitting in a pub, and trying to answer increasingly difficult questions about what I believed and why. I was quite frustrated with myself for not having all the answers. But perhaps giving the 'right' answers wasn't that important. After that discussion, my friends all seemed to respect my faith more, even if they disagreed with me. And it paved the way for many *more* conversations about God (most of which were also in the pub!). Evangelism can seem a little scary, but it really doesn't need to be. It turns out that the most important thing for me wasn't giving smart answers, but just being willing to spend time with my friends, be myself and share what I believed. Maybe that approach will work for you too.

In any case, if we truly believe the good news of the gospel, if we catch a glimpse of Jesus and see how amazing He is, surely we will be inspired to share this with other people. Notice how today's key verse uses the word 'will' – evangelism is a command; a compulsion and not an option. Of course, it's as we're filled with the Holy Spirit that evangelism becomes easier and more natural. But, even so, we must choose to take opportunities to share our faith, when those opportunities arrive.

Sometimes people go through life wanting the benefits of the Christian life without the challenges. They want a God who loves them and cares about them, but don't want to have to talk about that with somebody else! But the Bible is clear: we need to share our faith with others.

CHALLENGE

Who do you know who you could and should share your faith with? Make a list of five names. Pray for these five people every day. Then look for opportunities to talk to them (but don't force the issue if it's just not the right time) and trust God to give you the words to say.

READING Deuteronomy 5:1–21

KEY VERSE
v12 'Observe the Sabbath day by keeping it holy, as the LORD your God has commanded you.'

HAVE YOU EVER wondered why God bothered commanding us to take a day off? Why didn't He just suggest it? Why does this idea matter so much that God made it one of the Ten Commandments – the ten most significant commandments He gave us? (God's so keen on the idea of rest that He even commanded Israel to give the land a rest, not sowing or harvesting in a field for one year out of every seven! Exod. 23:10–11)

When I was at university, I wondered about exactly that. And I noticed that one of my friends never did any work on Sundays. At the time, I thought that was just a bit strange. I knew about the idea of a Sabbath but thought it was a little old-fashioned. That didn't still matter at the beginning of the twenty-first century, surely? Later, I found out the hard way why taking a Sabbath is really important. I'd been working hard for weeks, and this culminated in a training event on a Saturday. The event lasted all day, and I was then busy in the evening too. I woke up on Sunday morning feeling absolutely dreadful. I ached all over and felt exhausted. I realised I was on the verge of

making myself ill by over-working. I spent that day resting, not because I chose to, but because I had to! If I'd been wiser about taking time out to rest in the weeks before, I'd have been in a much healthier state.

God doesn't just tell us to rest on the seventh day because He thinks it's a nice idea. He gave us this commandment because He knows that we *need* to take a day a week to rest, for the good of our physical, mental and spiritual health. It doesn't necessarily have to be a Sunday, but we all need a day a week which is set aside for resting, spending time with God and having fun. God commands us to do this, not just for the sake of giving us a rule to follow, but because it's good for us. If we want to know God better and live His way, taking a Sabbath every week is a good way to start.

 CHALLENGE

Get your calendar out again. Set aside one day a week to relax, spend time with God and have fun. Don't let anything else interfere with this. Don't just think about it – do it!

READING Colossians 3:1–17

KEY VERSE
v17

'... whatever you do or say, do it as a representative of the Lord Jesus ...'

DAY 13

44

WHY ARE YOU here? What made you apply for this course at this university? Maybe you feel a real sense of purpose in what you're studying. You're doing this course to gain some expertise and then you're going to go out and change the world. Or maybe you're not so sure. Maybe this wasn't the course you really wanted and you just ended up here through Clearing. Or maybe you're not really sold on the whole uni thing at all and you just applied because it seemed like the thing to do.

But have you thought about what God might have to say about all this? If you're sure you know where your course and your life are heading, then good for you. But has it occurred to you that God might be interested in what you're doing now, not just in three or four years' time? And if you feel like you've drifted into uni life, do you wonder if God might have been the one who put you where you are? The truth is, regardless of how happy and settled and purposeful you may feel, God is interested in what you're doing and He wants you to represent Him here and now.

Everything you do is an opportunity to do that. Your course is important, obviously. It's a great chance to learn and stretch yourself academically and God wants you to work hard at your studies, as if you were working just for Him (Col. 3:22–24). But the same is true of everything else you do with your time. When you're with your friends, playing sport, cooking or at Student Union meetings, you can represent Jesus there too. Jesus can reach your friends and your campus and reveal Himself to them, *through you*.

Colossians 3 has a lot to say about exactly how we can represent Jesus too. It means we need to watch our lifestyle, give up bad habits and choose to be kind and forgiving. Above all, to represent Jesus, we must choose love (v.14). We must accept the love that God offers us and choose to share that love with the people around us. It's that love for God and for other people that should motivate everything we do and say. However happy you are with your university and your course, choose to love and choose to represent Jesus. If you do that, God can work through you and change you, your friends and your university.

 THINK

How can you represent Jesus where you are? Who exactly do you need to love? What will that mean for you in practice?

READING Jeremiah 33:1–11

 KEY VERSE
v3 'Ask me and I will tell you remarkable secrets you do not know about things to come.'

WHEN I WAS about seven, I wanted to be a pilot. By the time I was thirteen, I'd changed my mind. I wanted to be a journalist. Or maybe a barrister. When I got to filling in my UCAS form, I didn't really know any more what I wanted to do with my life. So I just chose to study a subject I enjoyed. (Looking back, that probably wasn't a bad decision.) Not much changed during my three years at uni and, with graduation looming on the horizon, I realised I had no idea what I should do next. I had no sense of purpose and no idea what God was doing or what He was leading me to.

In a small way, I can relate to how Jeremiah must have felt. He was in prison, his city was about to be destroyed, his people were going to be captured and taken into exile and he must have wondered what on earth God's purpose was in all this. How could God possibly bring something good out of this situation? But, although Jeremiah's immediate future looked horribly bleak, God reassured him that ultimately His plans were good. He and his nation would be healed, restored, forgiven and at peace, *if* they were willing to live God's way (vv.6–11). In the meantime, God was still with Jeremiah to comfort him, guide him and give him wisdom (v.3).

It seems rare that God will drop a fully-formed plan for someone's next twenty years into their lap. And, even if He does, He doesn't seem to be in the business of giving us an easy, problem-free existence. For a lot of us, life includes a fair amount of confusion, frustration and head-scratching. But in all this, we can still be confident that God's purpose is to heal us, restore us, forgive us and give us His peace. His plans for us are good! And even if we can't see exactly what those plans are and how God is going to get us there, He is always with us to guide us and give us His wisdom. It's been ten years since I graduated and I'm still not entirely sure where God will take me in the end. But He's always shown me the next step forward. And He's always been with me.

 PRAY

Commit your future to God. Let God speak to you about where you should go and what you should do. Give Him time and space to 'tell you remarkable secrets you do not know about things to come'.

MY STORY

BEING DROPPED OFF in a city where you know no one, with everything you know as normal being whisked away as your family leave, is a pretty daunting prospect. Freshers' Week in theory is a pretty brutal way to begin university life. A week of hardcore drinking with people you've only just met, in a city you hardly know, is certainly a challenge in living out your Christian faith. One night in Freshers' Week I went out with my flatmates and one of my friends brought back a girl to sleep with. I was reminded that God doesn't want us to judge the people around us but to love them. The whole Freshers' Week experience really tested the strength of my faith.

As far as church goes, I followed the crowd, going to a huge church along with hundreds of other students. But God's plan is different for everyone and despite the great teaching at this church, I knew it wasn't where God wanted me to be. It was hard to

go where God wanted me, rather than where a lot of my friends were. At times, I thought how much easier it would be if I wasn't a Christian: I wouldn't have to find a church, drinking could continue until I was totally smashed – I would be what the world would define as 'normal'. However, God had placed me at this university, in this flat, and in a specific church for a reason and I knew I had to carry out *His* plan for me. He never said it would be easy.

Before moving away I totally underestimated the power of prayer, but I found that in the first few weeks at uni I was talking to God just as much as I was speaking to other people. Through prayer, I was able to find a church that I love, find Christian and non-Christian friends and generally live in a godly way. My faith has certainly been stretched, but I know God has good plans for me and I know I can trust Him.

Beth, student at Newcastle

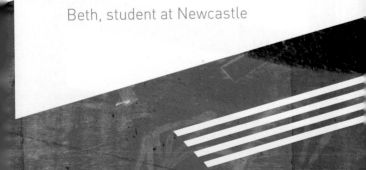

WHAT'S THE BEST THING ABOUT UNI?

'I like being part of a community. Hundreds of ace people who you know and the feeling of all being in it together.' **(Phil, Sheffield: Law)**

'Freedom! Buying whatever food I fancy at the supermarket. Meeting new people and being challenged by their opinions.' **(Sarah, Greenwich: English Literature)**

'Sports!' **(Tony, Leeds: Biochemistry)**

'The freedom to take responsibility for my own decisions and to make things happen for myself.' **(Rich, York: Linguistics)**

'Independence, managing my own time, opportunities.' **(Nicola, Cambridge: Music)**

'Meeting international students.'
(Lawrence, Reading: Geography)

'Learning things and feeling clever.'
(Jen, Newman College, Birmingham: Education)

'Free cheeseburger with a large meal at McDonalds!'
(Clive, Aberystwyth: Biochemistry)

'Discovering the person I truly am.'
(Emma, Wolverhampton: Special Needs and Inclusion)

'The work. Seriously, I love studying!'
(James, Queen Mary, London: Physics)

SECTION 3

LIFE

TYLE

LIFESTYLE MATTERS, NOT JUST BECAUSE OF THE EFFECT IT CAN HAVE ON YOUR WITNESS TO NON-CHRISTIANS, BUT SIMPLY BECAUSE AN UNHEALTHY LIFESTYLE IS BAD FOR YOU! SECTION 3 UNPACKS SOME GODLY ADVICE ON WHAT A HEALTHY LIFESTYLE LOOKS LIKE.

YOUR
LIFE-
STYLE

YOUR

LIFESTYL

TIP 1

Look after yourself – I don't want to sound like your mum, but make sure you take care of yourself! In all the excitement, eating right, getting enough sleep and taking exercise can get forgotten. The problem with that is that by the time you get to reading week, you'll be exhausted, out of shape and probably ill. Resist the temptation to stay up all night. Join at least one Athletic Union club. And, if the campus food and your cooking skills aren't up to much, get some vitamin tablets.

21

TIP 2

Don't drink too much – OK, I probably do sound like your mum now. I'm not saying you shouldn't enjoy yourself. What I'm saying is that overdoing it is a bad idea. Heavy drinking won't just give you a headache you'll want to forget, it'll also make you skint in a hurry. Don't feel you absolutely have to spend every evening in the union. If you do opt for a night out, alternate between alcoholic and soft drinks. And if you're running low on cash, spend it on food, not beer.

TIP 3

Set a budget and stick to it – This is a lesson I learnt the hard way. It's alarming how quickly the money can disappear. A new book here, a pizza there and one or two cappuccinos add up surprisingly quickly. It really is worth learning to manage your money. Make a note of what you spend your money on in the first month, then set yourself a budget based on that for the rest of the term. That's the easy bit. Now stick to that budget. Good luck!

14 –
RECOMMENDED
LIMIT ON UNITS
OF ALCOHOL
PER WEEK
FOR A WOMAN

KEY VERSE
v19 '... you are a slave to whatever controls you.'

ONE OF MY best friends in my first year drank an awful lot. I don't just mean he liked a drink. I mean he drank to the point where he fell over and passed out several times in our first term. On one night in Freshers' Week, we found him slumped over the end of his bed, still fully clothed. He hadn't even managed to shut his door before he lost consciousness.

It all might still have been OK for my friend if he had stopped drinking like that. The trouble was, he found he couldn't stop. He got so used to the drink that he found he needed it to get through a day. We could all see he had a serious problem – we just didn't know how to talk to him about it. While we were working out what to do, things were getting worse. My friend's mood was becoming increasingly unpredictable. I still remember the time he was thrown out of the union bar for peeing against the wall. He was struggling to concentrate in tutorials and started to fall behind in his studies. And his habit was getting so expensive he couldn't even afford to pay his rent. He was finally thrown out of our hall of residence for not paying his rent and he dropped out of his course soon after.

We can sometimes get the impression that drink and drugs can make us free; that they will make life fun and exciting and set us free from stress and pressure. That's just not true though. A drink or two might be enjoyable enough, but when you wake up the next morning, your problems are still there and if you've overdone it you'll have a headache too. That's not all. As my friend found out, if we get into the habit of getting drunk or high, we can find we need it just to get through the day. If we get to that point, the drug isn't setting us free: it's mastering us and holding us prisoner. I don't think there's anything wrong with drinking in moderation. But don't look for freedom in the bottom of a bottle. There's only one place to look for freedom (see Galatians 5:1).

CHALLENGE

Take an honest look at your intake of alcohol and recreational substances. Is there anything you need to cut down on or eliminate altogether? Are you looking for freedom in Jesus or in a bottle?

KEY VERSE 'But you, lazybones, how long will
v9 you sleep? When will you wake up?'

I KNOW, I KNOW. Calling students lazy – what a cliché. But there's a serious point to this. Spending all day in bed seriously limits your life experience. There are people to meet, places to see, things to do, great inspiring works of art and literature to discover and a world to introduce to Jesus. So let's get out and explore! Students have enough idealism to want to make big changes in the world and enough time, energy and intelligence to really influence the way society is heading. So it's ironic that at the time of life when we're best placed to start a revolution, we're struggling to get out of bed!

On a more down-to-earth note, erratic sleep patterns can have a detrimental effect on our work. Some of my friends fell behind on their coursework and eventually dropped out of their courses because they slept all day and didn't get around to doing any studying. Spending too much time online, watching TV or playing video games leads to the same risk. You can end up spending so much time staring at a screen that you disengage from the real world. You might be able to cruise through your first couple of terms like this, but before long this approach will get you into trouble.

Just in case you think I'm playing the 'lazy' card too strongly, let's look at the other end of the spectrum. Perhaps you're not sleeping enough. With a demanding course, lots of friends to keep up with, loads of clubs and societies and a campus to tell about Jesus, maybe sleep is slipping down your list of priorities. If that's you, be careful. Not enough sleep is just as unhealthy as too much sleep. It'll affect your concentration, put strain on your friendships and threaten your physical and mental health. Of course God wants you to work hard and be His representative in your uni, but He's not a slave driver. He loves you and wants what's best for you. That includes sleeping well and eating a balanced diet too.

 THINK

Think about your sleep habits. Do you need to be more disciplined about sleeping at regular times? How can you make sure you get eight hours a night and still have time for your other commitments?

KEY VERSE
v24

'Don't you realize that in a race everyone runs, but only one person gets the prize? So run to win!'

IN MY FINAL year at uni, my housemates and I realised we were becoming couch potatoes. Three years of beer, pies, Playstation and not much exercise had taken their toll. So we decided to start running together. The first time we went running, I got about 400 metres from my front door before I felt sick and had to stop. But the second time, I made it slightly further and the third time, further still. It wasn't long before we all started feeling healthier and more energetic.

You've probably spotted that in this passage from 1 Corinthians, it's not really physical exercise that Paul is talking about. He's using the images of an athlete and a boxer to convey the idea of discipline and how important that is in our walk with God. But a part of that discipline is to do with how we treat our bodies. We've covered a number of issues around this already: sex, drink, drugs and sleep. We need to be disciplined in taking exercise too. Earlier in 1 Corinthians, Paul describes our bodies as being 'temples of the Holy Spirit' (1 Cor. 6:19). In other words, what we do with our bodies matters to God. We can't separate our bodies from our souls. Being disciplined and honouring God with our bodies is as important as honouring Him with our thoughts and words.

But what if you're just not the sporty type? I'm not saying you need to swim the Channel tomorrow, if that's not your thing. If you know you're a bit out of shape, starting gently is the best idea. Walking or cycling instead of driving or getting the bus is a good start. And find something active that you enjoy. Play badminton with some friends, join the Hiking society or try rock climbing, for example. There are any number of ways to get active and if you can find something you really enjoy, you'll be far more likely to stick at it and get in shape. If you make the effort to get active, you'll feel better in yourself and you'll be honouring God while you're at it.

PRAY

Ask God to help you honour Him with your body. If you know you've been lax on this front in the past, take the opportunity to say sorry and ask God to forgive you.

I KNOW CHRISTIANS who love to go out clubbing. I also know Christians who wouldn't be seen dead in a club and are horrified that other Christians would even think about going there. Who's right? On one hand, if you just enjoy dancing and spending time with your friends and you're not there to get drunk and pair off with a stranger, what's wrong with it? On the other hand, some pretty crazy stuff goes on in nightclubs and is that really the kind of thing you want surrounding and influencing you? There's a lot to be said on both sides of the argument. But then again is it an argument worth having? Lengthy debates about the morality of clubbing can cause unnecessary rifts in churches and Christian Unions and surely there are more important things to do with our time, anyway.

For the Christians Paul was writing to, the debate wasn't about clubbing, but about meat. Most of the meat available would have been sacrificed to idols before going on sale. Some Christians therefore steered clear of meat, because they didn't want to do anything which might validate idol worship. Others reasoned that Jesus redeems all things and that because of Him we're living by grace not by rules, so ate whatever they wanted. There was no clear 'right' or 'wrong' answer, so Paul tried to discourage the church from arguing about it. The principle he emphasised was to 'aim for harmony in the church and try to build each other up' (v.19).

Perhaps we should take this principle on board too. If you enjoy clubbing, then go clubbing. But don't keep going on about it in front of other Christians, if you know they're uncomfortable with it. And if you're not sure nightclubs are the kind of places Christians should be, then stay away from them. But don't pass judgment on other Christians who don't see a problem with it. We don't want to risk damaging other people's faith by either condemning them or influencing them to do something they don't think is right. Instead, let's focus on how we can encourage each other to know Jesus better and follow Him more closely.

 THINK

Do *you* think it's OK for Christians to go clubbing? Why? How are your views and behaviour in this area affecting other Christians? Do you need to make any changes?

'I will pour out a blessing so great you won't have enough room to take it in! Try it! Put me to the test!'

ONE OF THE most stressful aspects of student life is handling money. Come to think of it, that's one of the most stressful aspects of life in general. You might think you're struggling to make ends meet. You might well be right. That's before we start thinking about paying off the student loan too. Unfortunately, you're likely to be paying that off for a good few years. So how can we be expected to give money away when we've got so little to start with?

This is about priorities. How we use our money generally reflects what we think is important. Usually, the more we spend on a particular thing, the more important we think that thing is. If we see God's work as important, that should be reflected in our bank statements. Of course you're not in a position to give hundreds of pounds a month to your church or other charities, but how are you using what you have? I expect you could afford to give at least £5 or £10 a month without too much trouble. It just means one or two fewer lattes a month, for example. And, if we develop good habits with our money now when we don't have much of it, we'll also handle it wisely in the future when we're better off.

When you read these words from Malachi, you can almost hear him tearing his hair out. God had showed Malachi that His people had been deliberately holding back money which God deserved. Because of that, they seemed to have been struggling with bad harvests and not enough food. Even more frustrating for God and for Malachi, the people were missing out on huge blessings. If they were willing to give God the money and resources He deserved, He promised He would provide everything they needed and more besides. I doubt you've been deliberately disobeying God like the Jews were, but there is a definite link between giving to God's work and receiving God's blessings. It might not necessarily mean God will give us more money, but prioritising God's work is always a wise move.

However much money we have, when we give our time, energy and cash to God, blessings will follow.

 CHALLENGE

Draw up a budget for the next month. Decide how you will spend your money and stick to the plan. Include how much money you will give to your church, your Christian Union and other charities. Then give that money straight away, before you're tempted to spend it on something else.

KEY VERSE
v16 'The servant who received the five bags of silver began to invest the money and earned five more.'

YOU MIGHT NOT believe it, but you have more free time now, as a student, than you're ever likely to have again. This time is a gift. How will you use it? Relaxing and having fun are good and healthy things to do, but there are so many other things you could do too. For example, you could get involved in student politics and make some changes to how your Student Union do things. You could help out with a children's group at your church. Or you could organise the Christian Union to start a project to help the homeless in your town.

The same thing goes for the long vacations. You could spend the whole summer resting and catching up with friends and those are both good things to do. But what an opportunity to do something different, challenging and valuable. Why not join a short-term overseas mission team or volunteer to help out at a Christian conference? Or perhaps get a job, pay off some of your loan and gain some valuable work experience for post-uni life.

When Jesus tells us something, it's probably important. When He tells us the same thing twice, it's definitely worth paying attention. In this case, He tells us the same thing three times in a row, which should really make us sit up and take notice! In verses 1–13, Jesus tells a parable which underlines how important it is to use what we have well. In verses 14–30, He tells another parable with the same point. In verses 31–46, He goes on to make a very similar point again. The chapter as a whole gives us a very strong and very challenging message: we have a responsibility to honour God with the gifts He has given us. That includes our time. I'm not saying we should overload ourselves with commitments, but we should certainly be committed to a few specific activities which serve other people in Jesus' name. How can you honour God with the time and gifts He has given you?

CHALLENGE

Are you honouring God with your spare time? What do you have planned for your summer break? How can you use your spare time and your vacations to serve God and help other people? Think about it, pray about it, then commit to one or two particular things.

KEY VERSE
v21 'Go and sell all your possessions and give the money to the poor, and you will have treasure in heaven.'

CHRISTIANS CAN BE very quick to soften what seems a very harsh lesson from Jesus in this chapter. Conventional thinking is that Jesus couldn't possibly really expect us to sell everything we have. He must have just challenged this one particular person to do that, because He knew that the guy loved his possessions and He wanted to challenge that. Maybe that's right. For sure, there's a challenge in this chapter that we should put Jesus first and not hold on to anything else so tightly that it keeps us from following Him.

But maybe there's more to it than that. What if Jesus actually meant every word He said here? What if we actually did sell everything we had and gave the money away? Is there any real reason we shouldn't take Jesus literally? There are groups of Christians in the world who have done that. They've sold their possessions, moved into a house together and now share everything they have left. Check out http://www.thesimpleway.org for example. It's very challenging and very inspiring!

OK, so maybe that isn't for everyone. Maybe I'm being unreasonable in expecting people to do that (especially when I haven't done it myself). But maybe we shouldn't be so quick to explain away Jesus' words when we don't like them. In any case, these words from Mark are a profound challenge to us and our materialistic culture. Instead of always focusing on getting more 'stuff' and keeping up with the latest gadgets, let's think about what we can give rather than what we can get. It's very liberating to de-clutter and give away stuff we don't need. How much of the stuff in your room or your house do you really need? Are there people or charity shops you could give some of your things away to? Or even, taking it one step further, what if you gave away something you think you *do* need? There's great value in living simply. It can reduce our worry and stress and help us focus on what really matters. '... true godliness with contentment is itself great wealth' (1 Tim. 6:6).

 PRAY

Ask Jesus to give you *His* perspective on your money and possessions. Pray about how you could live more simply.

MY STORY

THE PEOPLE I met on my first day at university would become my closest friends throughout my three years at Keele. I was the only Christian in my circle of friends. They didn't fully understand what I believed and why, but they were more or less accepting of my faith and we had a good time together. I had been worried about going to uni, particularly about how non-Christians would take to me and how I could live in a way that honoured Jesus. Being around Christians at uni, both at church and on campus, helped me to stay grounded and I found that when I saw little of my Christian friends that was when it was harder to stay true to the things I believed. I got involved with a church off campus and the Christian Union on campus and these helped to keep my relationship with God alive.

There were of course times when in terms of my lifestyle, I didn't behave quite like I should have, but thankfully we serve a God of grace. One issue that I fought with was drinking too much on nights out. I rarely got too drunk, but it was a temptation. Looking back I realise that it was when I went out that I had the best chance of being a good witness to my friends, but when I did have too much to drink I found that distinctions between being a Christian and non-Christian were blurred. At those times, I didn't look very different from my non-Christian friends. I often justified it by saying that, if I didn't drink as much as them, my friends would relate to me even less. I told myself I could stay a Christian and behave just like them. This is rubbish. I can see that now. I should've been trying to be more like Jesus, even on nights out.

Fred, student at Keele

USE YOUR H

SECTION

4

YOUR

UNIVERSITY IS **AN OPPORTUNITY TO LEARN.**
YOU KNEW THAT, OF COURSE. BUT THAT OPPORTUNITY
GOES **BEYOND LECTURES AND TUTORIALS.** THERE'S
AN AWFUL LOT TO LEARN AND EXPLORE OUTSIDE OF
YOUR COURSE. **SO USE YOUR HEAD.**

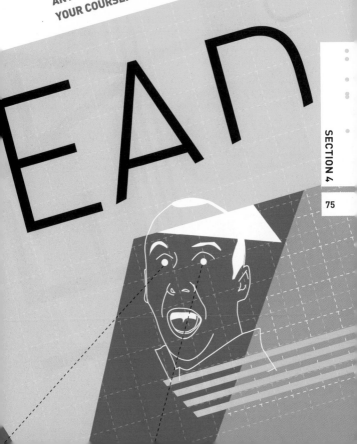

USE YOUR HEAD

USE YOUR HEAD

TIP 1

Read *anything* you can get your hands on – Your university is a gold mine of knowledge and exciting new ideas. Work hard for your course, but read wider than that. Find out more about science, philosophy, history, literature, art or anything else that catches your imagination. See a play or two and catch a few concerts. Feed your mind.

1 0 0 , 0

TIP 2

Talk to people who disagree with you – There should
be no shortage of them! Life is boring if we only
ever spend time with people who think like we do.
Talking to people who disagree with us on faith,
politics, science, economics or sport will make us
more rounded people and help us grow in our faith.
So don't run away from everyone who has slightly
different views from you; talk to them.

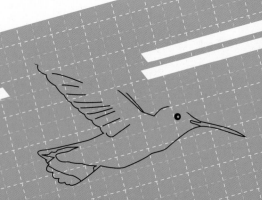

TIP 3

Pray – Finally, pray about all this. It's great to have a hungry, open mind, but don't let your mind be so open that it absorbs everything without thinking it over. Reflect on what you're seeing and hearing and pray about it. Ask God to give you His wisdom and discernment about what's good and godly, and what would take you on a path away from Him. Give Him time and space to speak and guide you.

KEY VERSE
v7 'Getting wisdom is the wisest thing you can do! And whatever else you do, develop good judgment.'

I ONCE HAD a boss who was very easy-going whenever I made a mistake. He'd help me sort out the mess I'd made, then shrug and say, 'Every day is a school day.' I knew what he meant. All of life is an opportunity to learn. Every experience – even a mistake – can teach us wisdom and good judgment. University is exactly the same. Of course you know you're there to learn. But my point is, your learning won't be limited to lectures and tutorials. You'll be surrounded by interesting people with challenging points of view, books to read, art and music to discover. You might even have the chance to go overseas or take a work placement as part of your course. All these things will develop you, make you a more rounded person and grow your wisdom. Not to mention the life lessons you'll learn from doing your own cooking and laundry and sharing a house. It's worth bearing in mind, though, that these things will only teach you if your mind is open and you're willing to learn.

Taking it a step further, be ready to grow in your faith and learn from the Christians around you. Be open to slightly different interpretations of the Bible. Watch

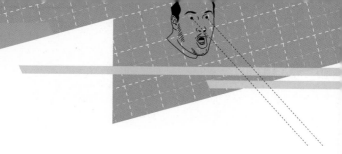

the lifestyle of the Christians around you too, and learn from their example. I'm not saying you should simply soak up everything you see and hear and accept it without thinking. That would be far from wise. Think about these things, pray about them and draw your own conclusions. But remember that your time at uni will be packed with opportunities to learn and develop your knowledge and your wisdom. Don't miss out on these opportunities! As the writer of Proverbs knew, wisdom is crucial. Wisdom will help you live your life in a healthy and godly way. Whatever else university throws at you, don't miss the chance to get wise. God gives wisdom to anyone who asks (James 1:5). But are you asking God for wisdom? Are you open to the different ways in which this wisdom can come?

 PRAY

Lord God, thank You for giving to anyone who asks, without finding fault. Thank You for university and all the opportunities it will give me to learn and grow in wisdom. Please use all my experiences to give me Your wisdom and help me live Your way. Amen.

📖 **KEY VERSE**
v7

'The LORD told Gideon, "With these 300 men I will rescue you and give you victory over the Midianites. Send all the others home."'

THIS MUST HAVE looked crazy to Gideon. Taking on a vast enemy with 32,000 soldiers is brave enough. Fighting with only 10,000 soldiers makes victory very unlikely. With 300 it's a suicide mission! What on earth was God doing? We don't know exactly what would have been going through Gideon's head as he saw his soldiers turn away and head for home in their thousands, but I think it's a fair guess to assume he was nervous! (He certainly needed some convincing to lead Israel in the first place – see Judges 6:36–40.) What we do know is that, whatever his own ideas were, he trusted God and went along with His plan. The result was an incredible victory.

Contrast this with how the Jewish leaders responded to the growing Church hundreds of years later. (Have a look at Acts 4:1–22, for example.) Like Gideon, they probably had their own ideas about the wisest way of doing things and about how God works. Unlike Gideon, they couldn't handle the idea that God might want to do something different. They had something extraordinary going on under their noses, with the Christians healing people with God's power and sharing the good news about Jesus. But

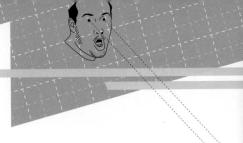

these things were so far outside the Jewish leaders' experience and understanding of God, that they couldn't believe God could really be at work in this way. So, they tried to stop it by arresting Peter and John and threatening them.

So when we see or hear God at work in a new and surprising way, we have a choice. Will we trust God that what is happening is important and valuable? Or will we distance ourselves from the whole situation? In the next few years, you'll see and hear some things that won't immediately fit your ideas of who God is and what He does. Sometimes, you'll be right to be cautious about these things. But don't dismiss anything out of hand. Pray about what you're seeing and hearing, be open to a new understanding of God and let Him speak to you about what's going on.

 THINK

When did you last see or hear something that didn't tie in with your view of God? How did you respond to this? Looking back, could there have been something true or valuable in it?

READING 1 Peter 3:13–18

KEY VERSE
v15
'And if someone asks about your Christian hope, always be ready to explain it.'

I WAS AT the bar, waiting to be served. It was quite busy, so I had to wait a while. While I was waiting, a friend arrived and stood at the bar next to me. We exchanged the usual pleasantries and then there was a lull in the conversation. After a pause, my friend was the next to speak.

'Why are we here?' he asked. To start with, I didn't understand what he meant.

'Well,' I replied, 'I'm here for a pint.'

That wasn't what he was getting at. He didn't just want to know why we were in the pub. He wanted to know why we were on the earth at all. I'd come for a drink, but my friend wanted to talk about the meaning of life! I wasn't expecting this, but it was an opportunity to share my faith. So I mentally said a lightning-fast prayer, opened my mouth and went for it.

We can never anticipate when we will get opportunities like this. Our friends won't just want to talk about God at Christian Union events or other times when we feel ready. The conversation could come any time, any place, whether you're prepared or not. I think this is why Peter urges us to 'always

DAY 24

84

be ready to explain' what we believe. It's important to be ready to share your faith, whenever it comes up in conversation. An important step in this is to know what you believe and why you believe it. If a friend asks you why you believe the Bible is true, you need to be ready with a decent answer. If they ask you why you don't get drunk or sleep around, it's fine to say, 'I don't think it's right', but you can bet their follow-up question will be, 'Why?' How would you answer that?

That's not to say we should reduce our faith to a set of intellectual ideas. It's very valuable to share our experiences of God as well as truths about Him. But people will ask us tricky questions, often at times when we're not expecting them. Let's be ready to talk.

 CHALLENGE

Do some thinking and praying about what you believe and why you believe it. You might find it helpful to read up on some apologetics too – books and articles that give intelligent reasons for what Christians believe. Don't be satisfied with glib answers. Be honest, be inquisitive and be ready to talk.

KEY VERSE
v27

'And the men, instead of having normal sexual relations with women, burned with lust for each other.'

WHEN PEOPLE FIND out you're a Christian, there are some hot topics that are bound to come up in conversation sooner or later. Homosexuality is a controversial issue, particularly in a university setting, where a homosexual lifestyle seems so widely accepted. So it's important to know what you believe about homosexuality and why.

Romans 1 discusses homosexuality at length. First, Romans 1 – and in fact the Bible as a whole – certainly does not say that God hates gay people. His love is endless and reaches everybody, regardless of age, race, gender or sexuality. The Bible does not say that homosexual practice is any more or less of a sin than anything else. Paul puts homosexual practice on a par with greed, envy and gossip (v.29). If we've done any of these things, we need God's forgiveness, but they're all equally forgivable.

So what *does* the passage say? In a nutshell, when we start ignoring God, we lose sight of the wisest, healthiest way to live (vv.18–23). If we ignore God, He lets us go our own way. When that happens, we can soon find ourselves getting involved in all sorts of things that damage us. This can include homosexual practice and also a whole list of other unhelpful

stuff (vv.29–31). Homosexuality isn't something that
defines a person and it isn't a natural and integral
part of who a person is. It's a distortion of who
that person was created to be, in the same way as
struggling with any other kind of temptation is.

So if we struggle with homosexual urges, Jesus
can set us free from them. Really? What about people
who desperately want to follow Jesus, but can't seem
to shake off their homosexual urges, however much
they pray about it? Is it OK for people in that position
to act on their homosexual urges? Should they just
be celibate? Or should they continue to pray until the
homosexual urges fade? This isn't an issue with an
easy answer. Think it over, pray it over and make up
your own mind.

 PRAY

Pray about the issue of homosexuality. If you know
anyone in particular who identifies themselves
as homosexual, pray about how to relate to this
person. Continue thinking and praying and never
forget that Jesus loves and accepts anyone,
regardless of their sexuality.

KEY VERSE 'This God, whom you worship without
v23 knowing, is the one I'm telling you about.'

THE WORLD PAUL lived in had numerous gods. Romans
(and in this case Greeks) believed in and worshipped
dozens of different beings. In this kind of environment,
how could Paul communicate the good news and show
that God is the only one worth worshipping, rather than
being just one god among many?

Our culture is very similar. There are millions of
people in the UK alone who worship any number
of other gods or no god at all. So we face the same
challenge Paul did. Living out our Christian faith in
this environment is not easy. Like Paul, we must try
not only to defend our beliefs when people around us
think we're wrong or misguided, but to actively share
our faith and to show that Jesus is the one true God.

Since our situations are so similar, it's well worth
looking at how Paul responded to this challenge.
First, when Paul shares the good news, he starts
where the other people are. He's not afraid to
talk about their beliefs – even though they're very
different from his own – before he ploughs on talking
about his own. Next, importantly, he's discerning
enough to see where God is already at work in this
culture. The altar dedicated to 'an Unknown God'

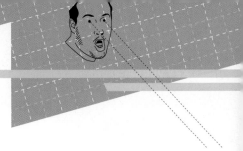

shows Paul that the Athenians are searching for God and want to know Him, even though they don't know Him at this point (vv.22–23). Following on from this, Paul sees an opportunity to share what he believes (vv.24–31). The response to Paul's message is very enlightening too. Some of the people he was talking to do become Christians. Others laugh at him. But there's a third group: people who aren't ready to become Christians, but want to spend more time with Paul and find out more.

As we interact with people of other faiths (or no faith), some may laugh at us. Some others may become Christians. But my guess is there will be a lot of people who fit into the third category – they won't be ready to become Christians, but they will want to keep talking. Let's be ready to invest in relationships with people like this.

 CHALLENGE

Be prepared for dialogue with people of other faiths. Don't always aim to win an argument. Just spend time with them, listening as well as talking. Pray that Jesus will guide your conversations.

KEY VERSE
v19 'You made the moon to mark the seasons, and the sun knows when to set.'

BELIEVING IN JESUS as our divine Creator isn't just a nice idea to make you feel warm and fuzzy. It makes sense. John describes Jesus as the 'Word' (John 1:1). In the original Greek, the word is *Logos*. It conveys logic and rational thought. God isn't an impersonal force, and He doesn't just give us a warm, fuzzy feeling. He thinks things through. The world has order and pattern because of God's rational intelligence.

If God embodies this kind of intelligence, we should show it too. Our faith must also have a solid, rational basis, and we must be ready to have some calm, rational discussions with people who disagree with us. For example, you'll probably meet some very intelligent people who think science and faith in God are incompatible. We have to be ready to discuss what we believe and why with people who hold this view.

About 700 years ago, people thought that the Sun orbited around the Earth or even that the Earth was flat. These beliefs were partly because people read verses in the Bible like today's key verse, and took them literally. The Bible has so much to teach us but, when we read it, we should remember what it is that

we are reading. The Psalms, for example, are poetry. Poetry includes images and symbolic language, which aren't meant to be taken literally. One thing the Bible is not is a science textbook. Our faith needs scientific knowledge to understand the universe as it is.

On the other hand, like a lot of poetry, the Psalms point to a profound truth beneath the imagery: God created the universe, and He controls the movement of stars and planets. He sustains the whole process, moment by moment, providing for all His creatures. Science alone won't tell us that. So science can tell us how the universe is structured, but only the Bible can explain why. Science tells us how the universe is, but faith gives an extra dimension of meaning to it. Faith in God interprets what science observes. Faith and science go hand in hand.

 CHALLENGE

How willing are you to discuss and explain your faith with people with differing views? Don't be afraid of this. Your faith won't collapse just because someone disagrees with you. Following Jesus makes sense!

KEY VERSE
v17 'As iron sharpens iron, so a friend sharpens a friend.'

THE METTLE GUIDE to *Starting University* finishes where it started – back in Proverbs, with verses that show us the value of good friends. Proverbs 27 emphasises the importance of a friend's advice (v.9), loyalty (v.10) and sensitivity to another's mood (v.14). But the most striking image this passage gives us is of two iron blades rubbing against each other, making each other sharper. This is what good friends can do.

During my year out, I regularly met up with a group of friends, to read the Bible, pray and talk. In some ways we were very similar and all wanted to serve God and know Him better. We shared struggles and I really valued the support, encouragement and prayer that my friends gave me. On the other hand, our personalities were quite different and we didn't always agree. We had some very stimulating and occasionally heated discussions. When iron blades rub together, sparks fly. The important factor in this is that we all put our friendships first rather than just trying to win the argument. The result was that we stopped arguing before we got to the point of falling out and we all

grew closer to God through being challenged to think about some of our views and behaviour.

Those friends kept me sharp. When I was struggling, they encouraged me. When I was apathetic, they fired me up. When I got funny ideas in my head, they put me straight. They helped me persevere in my faith, in every way they could. I urge you to find friends who can do the same thing for you. Think about who you can spend time with, reading the Bible, praying and sharing your struggles. If your Christian Union runs small groups, join one. If not, find other Christians in your hall or on your course and meet with them. Or look beyond campus and join a small group at your church. Whatever you do, find friends like these – soul friends – and hold on to them. They'll keep you sharp as you aim to live for Jesus, at uni and beyond. You can do the same for them too.

 THINK

Think and pray about who could be this kind of friend to you. Then go and find these friends, spend time with them and invest in your relationships with these people.

MY STORY

I KNEW I'D enjoy the social side of uni. Weeks before, I was already planning what I'd sign up to – Tap-dancing, Fencing, Christian Union, Amateur Dramatics, Cheese Appreciation Society – there were endless, hilarious possibilities and, when Freshers' Week finally arrived, I wasn't disappointed.

What took me completely by surprise was how much I LOVED the academic part too; using my head was so stimulating!

I remember the first time I saw the main library. Standing on the floor dedicated to History, its thousands of books crammed along the shelves, I found myself with a crazy impulse to seize as many as I could physically carry and devour them. I was hungry for knowledge!

I began to read around my subject and throw ideas into tutorials. It was such fun – everyone brought different opinions to the table and it was challenging